ORGANIZATION
is

ORGANIZATION is

Kid Possible

on the way to an "A"

by

Alex Fleming & Ben Hodge

A PUBLICATION OF
The Kid Concoctions Company

CREDITS:
Authors: Alex Fleming and Ben Hodge
Cover Art: Rob Durr
Cover art Photography: Jack Dragga
Graphic Design: Laurence J. Nozik
Publisher: Kid Concoctions Company

The Kid Concoctions Company
14761 Pearl Rd. PMB #161
Strongsville, OH 44136

ISBN: 0966108892

Manufactured in the United States of America
10 9 8 7 6 5 4 3 2 1

Visit us online at:
www.organizekids.com
www.kidconcoctions.com

Notice: The information in this book is true, complete and accurate to the best of our knowledge. All suggestions and recommendations are made without guarantees on the parts of the authors or the publisher. The authors and publisher disclaim all liability incurred in conjunction with the use of this information.

Table of Contents

3. Self-Image

4. Consequences

5. Benefits

Acknowledgments

Thanks to all of our colleagues, friends, and family who have helped us to develop our educational skills. We would like to thank the following people who enabled us to create this book.

Stacey Armstrong	Ryan and Michelle Rupp
Ron Chidsey	Tim Ruese
Tina Cochran	Jane Salem
Marci Gibbon	Virginia Schofield
Todd Milkie	Linda Simon
Chad Pado	Kurt Thonnings
Ginette Quien	Sue Wilson
Charles Reich	Bob and Geri Zettler
Audrey Repp	Barb Zimmerman

We truly appreciate the enthusiasm and guidance John and Danita Thomas provided us with this project. Without their optimistic support, our strategies would have never been published.

Dedication

Ben Hodge's Dedications:

To my grandparents, Richard and Marilyn Hodge and Ray and Mary Smith, our family beliefs begin with you. I am blessed to have two sets of grandparents that both have over fifty years of marriage. Our family has learned a lot from your example.

To my parents, Paul and Sona Hodge, who taught me the true meaning of hard work. Thank you for being such great leaders, supporters and loving parents. You model for everyone the true meaning family.

To Robyn, my wife, I never thought I could love someone so much. You bring joy into my life everyday. Hailey has become a beautiful child because of what you have taught her. You are an inspiration to me, and she and I thank you for it.

To Hailey, my daughter, your mom and I love you so much. You bring me so much happiness everyday.

Alex Fleming's Dedications:

To my grandparents, Colomba and Jim Delmonte and Loretta and Dick Patton, you are models for true happiness and family values. I am blessed to have you in my life. Thank you for everything you have done for me and I love you.

To my parents, Sharon DelMonte and Tom Fleming, you have shown me the importance of responsibility, love and respect, but most of all you have always believed in me. No matter what happened you were always there for me and you still are today. I love you very much.

To Rosa, my wife, you are my best friend and together we have created a life filled with happiness, laughter and love. I look forward to growing old with you and I cherish every moment that we spend together. I love you with all my heart.

To my beautiful children, Domenic, Maria and Vincent, whose smiles brighten my every day. You are my inspiration and I love you more than words can describe.

Preface

When I think of disorganization I think of a messy desk or a person who can't find anything. That person is not always a child. Adults are not immune to this problem, and I'm aware of this because I was one of those adults years ago. When Ben and I began writing this book, I tried to recall the points in my life when organization became a priority. Along the way I learned how to pass these necessary skills to my students.

When I graduated from college, I believed I was an organized individual. I was a reliable person who always had things done on time. My first job was teaching social studies and language arts to sixth graders. I immediately began planning lessons and units that would engage the students in the material. It was an exciting adventure. Everyday brought new challenges and this is when my organizational problems began to surface. Between teaching the material, keeping up with my grades and notes, helping students with emotional/social problems, and professional development…I was swamped!

So I came up with an idea. I should take night classes to get my graduate degree! Maybe I can sharpen my skills to help me in the classroom or I would just go crazy from being too busy. As I began classes I noticed that this just compounded my problem of disorganization and made it more apparent I needed help.

It never occurred to me that I had tremendous resources at my fingertips. The colleagues in my building! Young teachers usually think they know all the latest methods to be successful in the profession, but I got over that misperception rather quickly. I began to ask the experienced colleagues many questions, became a great observer of their methods, and tried to help in every way possible to learn how to master this "OR-GAN-I-ZA-TION" thing. Let me tell you…they were organized! They had binders, folders, tabs, dividers, etc… for everything. You could ask them for anything and they would pull it out at a moment's notice or would tell you exactly where it was.

It quickly became apparent to me that they had very organized students. The kids had different binders for each class that were color coded and organized to separate notes, homework and other important papers. They were ready to go at all times and really retained a tremendous amount of what was being taught.

Ben Hodge was one of my fellow teachers, and he is one of the most organized professionals I have ever observed in my life. He showed me how to organize my materials, time, schedule, and how to teach those important skills to my students. As we worked together for the next few years, we began developing many strategies to help improve our students' organization. We used input from students, parents and other teachers to find what worked best for the young adults in our lives. We began implementing those strategies into our classrooms.

What we found was amazing. We organized our students as well as their parents. We also found that our students' achievement, self-esteem, and learning increased. When Ben left teaching to become a principal, we decided to put our procedures and strategies down on paper for our students and parents to use. It occurred to us that there are thousands of kids and parents that can benefit from this knowledge…the knowledge of how to get organized!

What Is It?

Parents of children who are disorganized usually try to fix the child themselves, but it is often hard to identify the source where the child learned disorganization skills. Organization and disorganization are learned habits. A learned habit means one has been taught how to be organized...or disorganized. In the same way you teach a child to be organized, it is possible to teach an individual to be disorganized.

The parent's responsibility is to determine the source of this learned behavior. In many cases the parents themselves are disorganized. Are we saying you intentionally taught your child how to be sloppy, careless and irresponsible? No. Parents don't always realize they are constantly modeling behavior for their children. Think about it... they watch and mimic everything you do. Ben and I truly believe the major part of parenting is modeling. Do you have papers everywhere or cannot find that bill that was supposed to be mailed out last week? Is your child's book bag a mess? They are doing what you have modeled. If you have no organizational system, then they won't either. When you begin to correct your own behavior, include your child in the process. They will see the priority of organization, and how important it is to you.

Be sure that you are modeling the behavior that you want for your child. If you want your child to say "please" and "thank you", then as a parent it is your job to always say "please" and "thank you." The same idea applies to organization. If you model the desired behaviors, your child will learn how to be organized.

OTHER CONTRIBUTING FACTORS

There are other contributing factors to disorganization from what we have observed. Mainly students with: Attention Deficient/Hyperactive Disorder, learning or emotional disabilities, family tragedy, etc. We have also been very successful in using our strategies with these children.

CHAPTER 1

Home Environment

Structures/Schedules

*Every year a teacher has a student who is academically incon-
sistent. One year I had a student by the name of Timmy who
was a pretty good kid. He got B's and C's, but still academically underachieved for his abilities. I could not determine
the reason for his inconsistency until our fall conference day.
After brainstorming with his mother why the strategies that we
had tried did not work, it came to me. His mother continued
to complain about the nightly "battle" to do homework. She
said that by the time he finally sat down and started working, it was already late in the evening. The entire family was
stressed out over the "battle." I asked her to describe to me a
typical night. She claimed it was due to the fact that he came
home from school and snacked, played, called friends, etc. He
kept avoiding the task of working on homework. Once she was
able to get him to sit down and work, he would use the bathroom, search for materials, or do anything possible to avoid his
work. I decided that she needed to structure her time at home
better with Timmy. The next day Timmy, his mother, and I
sat down and devised a schedule that he was to follow at home
each night. His goal was to be more successful in school by following the schedule. At first, Timmy thought he would lose all
his free time and not ever get to play. Three weeks later our
team met again to discuss Timmy's progress. Timmy said that
he loved the schedule because he had more free time to play
and his grades improved. Mom was excited as well because
there were less "battles" and the whole family was happier and
more relaxed. Timmy stuck to the schedule and modified it
over the next few years. He and his mother continue to practice this daily routine as Timmy becomes more successful and
independent.*

Some parents have no routines and are very unstructured in their everyday life. This isn't wrong, but don't expect your child to be structured and have set routines when it comes to organization. Structure is one key to organization.

What do you do when you come home from work? Do you go out to eat, do you eat in, do you do things spontaneously, or do you have a basic schedule? You don't have to own a calendar that specifically states that you must read from 4:00-4:30, take a bathroom break and then talk for 20 minutes. You do, however; need to have some basic structure. This is very predictable, but it makes organization easier for most people, especially children.

Kids want to know what is going to happen and how. In our first years of teaching, one question students would ask as they walked in our room was…"What are we going to be doing today?" It didn't take long for us to figure out they wanted to know the expectations and the "structure" for the class. Children feel the same way at home. Doing homework in the car, in between soccer practice and piano lessons (if you have time) is not very structured or conducive for learning. If your schedule changes from evening to evening and there is no consistency, then this may be a major contributor to your problem. A set schedule will help fix your organizational challenge. You may first imagine you and your child will hate this idea because it will seem as if there will be no free time. On the contrary, you will soon find tasks are efficiently completed which allows more free time.

Kids want to know what is going to happen and how.

A schedule conducive to learning

Giving yourself more than enough time to accomplish your set tasks for the day is the key to a good working schedule. Many people think the key term in that sentence is *enough*. It's not! *More* is the key word. If you give yourself more time to get to a destination you will rarely be late. If you give yourself more time to complete a task, you will always be done on time. Wouldn't you want to be known as a punctual and dependable person? Listed below are seven essential scheduling features you must accomplish to obtain a structured schedule:

GOAL

Begin by deciding upon a goal. Is your child's goal to stay organized in school? Is it to organize the hectic days and evenings or to get that big project done in a few weeks? You must be specific because your child's goal will drive the schedule.

VISUAL AID

Have a visual of your child's goal that you can put with the schedule. Whether it is a sample report card of straight A's or a motivational picture, have a visual as a reminder of why the child is making this change.

TASKS

Make a list of the NECESSARY tasks that must be done. These should include the tasks that cannot be deleted from a schedule and are hard to rearrange; therefore we will start with them. Some examples would be meals, homework, practice, etc. You can also list areas where your child needs improvement. Putting papers in the appropriate folders for homework, packing your book bag the night before school, checking for quality and accuracy would be examples.

TIME:

Write down how much time it takes to accomplish each task listed. Give your child more than ample time to complete the task. Don't forget to add time when transitioning from one task to another.

PRODUCTION

Create your child's schedule. Place the times into your child's schedule in the appropriate places. DO NOT combine tasks. For example, eating breakfast and driving to school should not be combined!

LEISURE TIME

If you have an open time, allow your child to decide what to do. Be careful not to plan every minute of a child's day. Kids today often don't know what to do when faced with "unscheduled" time.

CHECKING SCHEDULE

The final step is to have someone else check your child's schedule. You do not have to follow their advice, but just listen. They might remember something that you forgot or offer help. If you did forget something, it is not hard to fix. Take out a leisure activity and fill it with a necessary task.

You just prioritized your child's tasks and created a schedule. For reference we have included a blank schedule and an example on the next two pages.

SAMPLE SCHEDULE

Daily Schedule

GOAL: Complete Homework

Nightly

VISUAL AIDE

Necessary Tasks

NEED	TIME REQUIRED
Homework	55 minutes
Dinner	35 minutes
BBall Practice	90 minutes
Driving to/from	
Practice	15 minutes
Bed Prep	20 minutes
Chores	30 minutes

Schedule

TIME(S)	TASK
4:00 – 4:15	Leisure Time
4:15 – 5:10	Homework
5:10 – 5:45	Dinner
5:45 – 6:00	Drive to Practice
6:00 – 7:30	Practice
7:30 – 7:45	Drive from Practice
7:45 – 8:15	Chores
8:15 – 8:40	Leisure Time
8:40 – 9:00	Bed Prep
9:00	Bed Time

SCHEDULING TIP

For kids in pre-k to third grade you should include reading in your nightly schedule. This is crucial to developing your child into a fluent and independent fourth grade reader. This nightly practice should continue throughout their education.

BLANK SCHEDULE

Daily Schedule

GOAL: _____

_____

VISUAL AIDE

Necessary Tasks

NEED	TIME REQUIRED
_____	_____
_____	_____
_____	_____
_____	_____
_____	_____
_____	_____
_____	_____
_____	_____
_____	_____

Schedule

TIME(S)	TASK
_____	_____
_____	_____
_____	_____
_____	_____
_____	_____
_____	_____
_____	_____
_____	_____
_____	_____

To make your schedule more appealing you can write it on construction paper, cut out each task, laminate it, put magnetic tape on the back, and post the schedule on your refrigerator.

SCHEDULING TIP FOR FAMILIES WITH MULTIPLE KIDS
Create an individualized schedule for each of your children to follow. Then create a master schedule for the parent to follow. This will keep families on the same page and evenings/weekends will be less hectic.

ROOM ORGANIZATION

Why is it important that a child's room be clean and organized? The only thing children have ownership of is the materials in their room…clothes, bed, toys, etc. If children are not taught the value of their belongings at a young age, they will not value possessions as they get older. This lesson can be taught by teaching them how to have their belongings organized. Listed below are some room organization tips:

CLOTHES

Ninety percent of morning battles are due to picking out clothes for the day. Laying out the clothes the night before or laying them out for the week can eliminate this. The clothes laid out the night before can be placed on the dresser or the foot of the bed. Five shelves can be purchased and placed in the closet so you and your child can pick out clothes on Sunday together and lay them on each shelf.

CLOSET

Make it simple and accessible to them.

- Go vertical — use a closet 'rod doubler' to save space due to children's clothes being smaller. Hang "tops" on the top rod and "bottoms" on the bottom rod. Hanging storage bags work well as hanging shelves.

- Top shelf should still be accessible. Items not used every day should be placed on the top shelf. Clear containers and labels allow them to see what is inside without opening them.

- Shoes are the most difficult to place in a defined space because kids use them every day and don't take the time to put them

PRE-K PARENTING TIP

One factor that makes instilling organization in a pre-k child difficult is the child's inability to read. Listed below are some tips to help children recognize where their belongings are stored.

- Use Colored Labels
- Use Stickers with pictures
- Use basic letters or numbers for the containers (A,B,C or 1,2,3 etc…)

on a shelf or a cubbyhole. Baskets below their hanging clothes allow them to kick them off and into their designated space.

• Items that are used every day such as bathrobes, coats, hats, etc. can be placed on hooks so your child can grab and run.

Toy Organization

It is important to remember that children don't own many things. They view their toys as their own property and have their own set of rules or laws to protect their property. The laws that they follow are very specific....

1. If I like it, it's mine.

2. If it's in my hand, it's mine.

3. If I can take it from you, it's mine.

4. If I had it before, it's mine.

5. If it's mine, it must never seem to be yours in any way.

6. If I'm doing or building something, all the pieces are mine.

7. If it looks like mine, it's mine.

8. If I saw it first, it's mine.

9. If you are playing with something and you put it down, it automatically becomes mine.

10. If it's broken, it's yours.

You need to sort through the toys at least twice a year. One good time to do this is after the winter holiday season. You should decide whether you want to keep, store, donate or pitch the toys you have. It is a good idea to have a person with an unbiased opinion help you sort through the toys.

KEEP toys they play with every day

STORE toys with sentimental meaning that are too old to play with

DONATE toys that are in good condition that they don't play with anymore, toys that you have more than one set

PITCH broken toys, non collectable toys, toys that don't have the value to be donated

PARENT TIP

Pick a day each week (preferably Sat./Sun.) to have your child organize and clean the child's room and belongings. Your child may need to do this twice a week.

Study Space

The study space needs to be a place where your child can focus on the task at hand without interruptions. The study space does not necessarily have to be the child's room.

- No television and minimal distractions (Light instrumental music or a fan running in the background might help students with ADD/ADHD focus.)
- Materials/supplies need to be in easy access of the study space
- A table or desk that is large enough to have two students do their work

They need this room so they can put other assignments or necessary supplies to the side

They need this room so a parent can assist with homework

They need this room so a parent can read a magazine or do bills to model work time behavior

Time Management

Time management is pertinent to successful study habits. Waiting until the night before (cramming) will result in more stress and less retention of the material. Studying strategies are listed below for efficient use of time:

- Find out about tests/quizzes as soon as possible.

- Create an outline of the material that will be covered on the test or quiz. Some teachers may give this out as a study guide.

- Make a list of what you want to study for the night and set a time limit. Study every possible night before the test.

- Start with general topics and, as the test get closer, study the more specific topics.

- Review and make a sample test or quiz to practice.

- Increase skills with rote work such as memorizing vocabulary, dates, formulas, etc. By singing a song or creating game with family members, you can make rote work more enjoyable.

The student example on the next page was a quiz to ensure the students knew the oceans and continents. They were told spelling would count on the quiz. I remember asking her why she did so poorly on the quiz and her response was she didn't have time to study. This particular student was very disorganized when it came to time management. She was an above average student and very capable of acing this quiz. The bad grade on her quiz was an example of her not studying because it was obvious from her answers she knew the content.

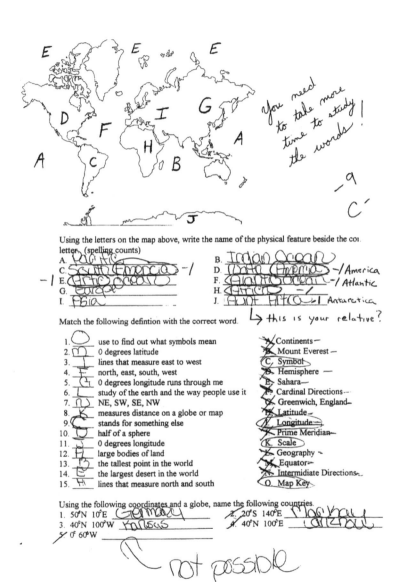

You need to take more time to study the words!

-9

C´

Using the letters on the map above, write the name of the physical feature beside the cor letter. (spelling counts)

-1

A. Pacific
B. Indian Ocean
C. South America -1
D. North America -/ America
E. Africa Ocean
F. Atlantic Ocean -/ Atlantic
G. Europe
H. Africa -/
I. Asia
J. North Africa -/ Antarctica

→ this is your relative?

Match the following defintion with the correct word.

1. ⟨O⟩ use to find out what symbols mean
2. ⟨M⟩ 0 degrees latitude
3. ⟨?⟩ lines that measure east to west
4. ⟨?⟩ north, east, south, west
5. ⟨G⟩ 0 degrees longitude runs through me
6. ⟨L⟩ study of the earth and the way people use it
7. ⟨?⟩ NE, SW, SE, NW
8. ⟨K⟩ measures distance on a globe or map
9. ⟨?⟩ stands for something else
10. ⟨?⟩ half of a sphere
11. ⟨?⟩ 0 degrees longitude
12. ⟨?⟩ large bodies of land
13. ⟨?⟩ the tallest point in the world
14. ⟨?⟩ the largest desert in the world
15. ⟨?⟩ lines that measure north and south

A. Continents —
B. Mount Everest —
C. Symbol
D. Hemisphere —
E. Sahara —
F. Cardinal Directions —
G. Greenwich, England —
H. Latitude —
I. Longitude —
J. Prime Meridian —
K. Scale
L. Geography —
M. Equator —
N. Intermidiate Directions —
O. Map Key

Using the following coordinates and a globe, name the following countries.
1. 50°N 10°E _Germany_
2. 20°S 140°E _Mongolia_
3. 40°N 100°W _Kansas_
4. 40°N 100°E _Arizona_
5. 0° 60°W _____

↖ not possible

CHAPTER 2

School
Environment

Material Organization

As a teacher and an administrator, I thought I had seen everything in school. One day one of my eighth grade teachers came up to me and said, "Mr. Hodge, there is a funny smell coming from Darlene's locker. You might want to check it out!" I immediately grabbed my locker key to investigate. I stopped by Darlene's class so she could help out with any problem that I might find. She opened her locker and revealed 15 pop cans, five sweatshirts, one winter coat and three furry, green (used to be brown) lunch bags. I noticed right away there were no school supplies. As she began cleaning her locker, I asked her where her books were. She was reluctant to tell me, but after further questioning, she said they were all over the building. I asked her to show me. As we traveled around the building, she opened every half locker that contained a fire extinguisher. Inside was the book and notebook for the class that was closest to the fire extinguisher. We gathered up all of her books and wiped out the locker. After a long discussion about fire extinguisher safety and the importance of material organization, we implemented strategies to help her become organized. I monitored her progress closely over the next few weeks. On the second to last day of school all the students cleaned out their lockers and turned in their books. As I walked down the hall, kids were throwing papers and notebooks in the trash. I walked toward Darlene's locker and she said to me,"Thank you, Mr. Hodge, for helping me this year." I said, "You're welcome," and peaked into her locker one last time. She had very little garbage or papers to throw away.

With your child you need to create a system that fosters organizational success. This section will help your child to develop physical organizational skills.

Your child may have never been taught, or understood, what it means to be organized. Knowledge of organization is essential for any child to be successful. Adults assume that children have previously been taught organizational skills and attribute disorganization to laziness or lack of motivation. In reality the child wants to be organized, but doesn't know how. If this is the case, the child needs to have a lesson on organization. Below are some methods we have implemented to physically organize kids:

COLOR CODING

It is easy with the supplies we have today to color code materials for your child. Each content area should be a different color. For example, red notebook/folder/ book cover should be for math, all social studies materials should be blue, etc. If your child's materials are all the same color for each content area, this makes it easier for them to:

• Grab their materials and go to class

• Place papers, notes, homework, quizzes in the correct colored notebook/folder

  It is important that math homework does not go with social studies, etc. They should NEVER have loose papers floating around.

• Place the correct materials in their book bag for homework

For a small percentage of students, the above system may be too overwhelming. If this is the case you may try a large 3-ring binder. You can buy folders and spiral notebooks that can stay in the 3-ring binder that is the color that matches the content area.

LABEL MATERIAL / DIVIDERS WITH HEADING

- Label all notebooks/folders with name and subject

- Label the binding on all books and notebooks so it can easily be seen in a locker

- Dividers should be placed in notebooks to separate notes/homework/quizzes and tests

TAKE-HOME FOLDER

The take-home folder should contain any graded work and notes to parents to keep the "lines of communications" open. The frequency in which the folder goes home depends on the child's grade level. The take-home folder should go home to the parent at least once a week. Middle school students should start to be weaned off the take-home folder so they are prepared for high school independence.

MATERIALS TIP
Paper folders tear easily. Plastic folders are more durable and can be purchased in place of paper folders.

SPIRAL NOTEBOOKS

Many teachers prefer homework turned in on loose-leaf paper. It is a good idea to strictly use a spiral for notes so they never get lost or disorganized.

ASSIGNMENT NOTEBOOK/PLANNER

- Assignment notebook is the equivalent to a planner/calendar for an adult.

- All assignments should be written down even if they are completed. Writing "done" is unacceptable. This makes the parents aware of all assignments.

- Use this as a daily communication tool between teacher and parent.

  If the child doesn't write down the assignments, ask the teacher to check the assignment notebook daily for completion and initial it. The parent can check the assignment notebook that night and initial next to the completed assignments.

BOOK BAG

- Children should clean their book bag at least once a week with your supervision.

- Take out all papers and review them with a parent.

- Place papers in appropriate place…notebook, trash, etc.

- Pack the night before to save time in the morning. This allows the child to double check for the correct materials for the next day.

LOCKER

- Coat and book bag should be hung up on the hooks.

- All books and binders should be labeled on the spine.

- Books should be standing on their edge so you can see the spine.

- Supply-box with crayons, markers, etc… should be stored in your locker.

- Should be cleaned out and organized once a week.

- Provide reminder lists to be placed in their locker. It can include items that need to be carried home each day. If they continue to forget key items, they should clean out their lockers or desks completely each night and bring it all home. A week of this and they will be willing to check the list each day.

- Locker shelves can be purchased to assist with organization.

Children should clean their book bag and locker at least once a week.

DESK

Your child's desk should be cleaned out and organized once a week. Listed below are the supplies that should be stored in your child's desk:

- Books, binders, notebooks that are needed for that classroom
- Assignment notebook
- Pencil/Pen
- Book to read once assigned tasks are completed

COMPUTERS/EMAIL

- Check homework assignments on-line if provided by the teacher
- Type out assignment

  If children have trouble with spelling/grammar or have illegible handwriting, they should type their homework. They will have access to a computer the rest of their lives. We have found this method improves spelling and grammar recognition.

- Email assignments to the teacher
- Ask homework questions on message board or instant messaging

  Instant messaging needs to be monitored closely for appropriate usage.

CORK BOARD/BULLETIN BOARD

- Hang this in the your child's bedroom on a wall so they can see it every day.
- Post goals and motivational materials on it.
- Post long term assignments on it.
- Post a school calendar.

After you establish some type of organizational skills, a vital element is to continually monitor it until it becomes habitual. These habits will not develop overnight. The first lessons need to be remedial. Many children think that if they have a folder for their papers, they are organized. Organization is a multi-step process. In our experience students of all abilities tend to struggle with multi-step processes. The resources in this book can be beneficial, however, keep in mind your child's teacher is one of the trained professionals in your child's life. They have been trained in child psychology, behavior modification and organizational strategies as well as many other areas involving education. They have experienced children with similar difficulties and have witnessed behaviors in your child that you may have overlooked. Remember that the environment at school is different than the environment at home. Consult them with any questions or concerns you may have about your child.

TEACHING TIP

As teachers we stress the importance of organization in our classrooms. One way that we did this was to spend 10 minutes a day on:

· Checking assignment notebooks
· Organizing binders and folders
· Cleaning lockers and desks

As a parent you should spend 10 minutes a day helping to organize your child's materials.

Little Johnny

When you think of a child's daily organization, what comes to mind? Some parents imagine little Johnny skipping down the street with his book bag full of his supplies and ready to tackle the daily assigned homework. Well, in many cases Johnny's book bag might be full, but not the way we think it should be. It's possible that he has a book, some paper (not in a folder of course), a gym shirt, and maybe a CD he promised to bring in for his buddy. Of course you're not aware of this when he comes home. Why? When you ask what he did at school today, his reply is, "Nothin'." "Do you have any homework?" you ask. "I finished all of it at school." He replies as he hurries out the door to his friend's house or downstairs to play on his new game system. No, no, no... in reality Johnny's nightly homework routine is as follows:

3 minutes getting his books out

12 minutes looking for the assignment

20 minutes explaining to his parents that the teacher is mean

7 minutes complaining that the assignment doesn't make sense

6 minutes for a bathroom break

15 minutes talking to a friend about the assignment

12 minutes getting a snack

10 minutes sitting at the table waiting for mom to do the assignment

These examples may seem funny or frighteningly familiar, but there is something you can do. This brings us to another key point...Responsibility.

Responsibility

It is your child's responsibility to bring home the necessary supplies along with an understanding of the assignment to complete it effectively. It is the parent's responsibility to make sure that the assignment is completed. Clever children will do whatever they can in order to shift the responsibility onto you or someone else. For example, your family uses the homework hotlines and websites created by the teacher. Are you using these resources to obtain the homework assignment or to check up on your child? If you are the one getting the assignments, then who is the one learning the responsibility? There are some simple solutions when children claim they didn't bring home the necessary supplies to do the homework. Below we have included some strategies you can incorporate to make your child more responsible.

How do you make your child more responsible? Making your child more responsible starts with follow-through. You have to start simple by giving them chores around the house. This is so you can monitor that they will carry out the task. It is important to encourage and give directions, but they must complete the task independently. What if your child came home unprepared to complete their homework assignment?

• Review what the child should bring home every day

• Do not take your child back up to school to get materials; do not take on their responsibilities. If your child consistently "forgets" to bring home materials, have the child bring home all materials in their locker every night. They can do this until they can handle the responsibility.

• The parent chooses a similar assignment. This assignment is not to be graded by the teacher but may be looked at to help you reinforce the correct behavior. Children must make up the missed assignment the next day when they get the appropriate materials. They will also have to suffer the natural consequences from the teacher such as a lower grade. Below are some content area lessons you can have your children do at night if they are unprepared to complete their homework assignments.

SOCIAL STUDIES

Ask your child the concept they are studying. Tell them to write a one-page paper on that concept.

LANGUAGE ARTS

Have your child write a one-page persuasive letter to the teacher explaining why it is their responsibility to be prepared to do their homework.

MATH

Direct your child to write out 20 addition, subtraction, multiplication or division problems for them to practice their computation skills.

SCIENCE

Have children in primary grades compare and contrast humans to fish. Depending on your child's skill level this can be written or be done verbally. Have children in intermediate grades compare and contrast the ecosystem of the ocean to the ecosystem of fresh water. Have children in middle school or high school write a one-page journal entry explaining the significance of each aspect of the scientific method. (Hypothesis, Procedures, Experiment, Data Collection, Analyze Data, Conclusion)

Making your child more responsible starts with follow-through.

Homework Independency

How do you teach your child to work independently on homework?

- Create a study space conducive to learning (refer to home environment).

- No TV, video games, phone calls or rewards of any kind until homework is finished. Be firm on this one.

- Classical/instrumental music can be played at a low volume while your child is working. Research has shown that this may help your child focus (especially children with ADD/ADHD).

- Determine a time every night that they will work on their homework.

- Teach them to take out their assignment notebook and prepare the necessary materials.

- For the first few weeks work intensely with them on homework checking for comprehension and completion.

> **PRIMARY PARENT TIP**
> If your child has assigned homework or has no homework, you should still read to your child each night.

- If homework can't be completed in one half-hour sitting, let them take short breaks. But allow no TV in between.

- After two weeks begin to just check for completion and see if they have any questions about the assignment. The most productive situation would be for you to sit next to your child and model the behavior you want them to exhibit. You can be doing bills, reading a book/magazine, writing a letter, etc…

This task needs to be something that can occupy your attention while your child is working.

This task must be inconsequential enough that you can stop what you are doing to help your child if they need it.

This task must not be a distraction to them.

- After four weeks begin to let the child complete their assignments on their own. Once again, it will be wise for you to sit next to your child and model the desired behavior. Ask your child if they need help, but be sure to give your child the opportunity to complete the assignment on their own.

- If after six weeks the child seems to regress back to incompletion of homework assignments, you should start this process over again.

TEACHING TIP

Intermediate and middle school grade children should select an age appropriate book for daily silent reading. Create a chart for you to initial that your child completed their silent reading for that day. Silent reading should be for 20 minutes a day. This can be done in school and the teacher can sign the chart.

As teachers we knew the importance of reading and therefore used the practice of silent reading on a daily basis.

Long-term assignments

The 6th grade student example on these two pages is an example of a long-term assignment that was obviously done the night before it was due. This report was actually assigned three weeks prior to the due date. Students were required to do research and the final copy was to be 1-½ pages in length.

DRAGONS

DRAGONS ARE MITHOLOKAL CREATURES.

DRAGONS ARE LIZARD LIKE CREATURES THAT
WOULD BREATH FIRE AND SCRACH.

THESE CREATURES WRE REPRESENTED WITH GOOD AND EVIL.

DRAGONS *were* ARE RULERS OF THE WORLD BAK IN THE MIDLE AGES.

PEOPLE WERE AFRAID OF DRAGONS IN THE MIDLE AGES.

THEY THOUGHT THEY WERE EVIL SPIRITS THAT HUNTED PEOPLE.

See me!

DRAGONS ARE MITHOLOKAL CREATURES.

DRAGONS ARE LIZARD LIKE CREATURES THAT WOULD BREATH FIRE AND SCRACH.

The child on the previous pages probably followed the guide-lines below for a long-term assignment.

Long-term assignments are given the night before they are due. This explains the name "long-term assignment." It is a long-term commitment that begins at 9:00PM and ends at midnight. It is important that the whole family be involved in the assignment. One family member must run to the store for a poster board, and another family member ends up in tears (does not have to be the student). One parent needs to stay up all night and complete the project. The other parent needs to call the student out sick. It is not necessary to have the student's name on the assignment.

Our guidelines below will eliminate the problems you read about in the above paragraph.

How do you teach your child to plan for long-term assignments?

• Understand the requirements and the expectations of the project completely before you begin to plan for the assign-ment.

• The teacher has given a due date, but to be efficient with your time management, you must have the project completed two days prior to that date. This is to eliminate unforeseen problems such as: power outage, printer runs out of ink, run out of supplies or your dog eats it.

• Once you know the due date, create an outline for project completion.

Long-term projects should be broken up into no more than four sections with completion dates. The completion dates should be spaced out evenly for the time that it takes to complete the proj-ect. Any more sections will make your child feel overwhelmed. An outline for long-term projects should be as follows:

Section 1: pre-write/brainstorm
Section 2: write/assembly
Section 3: edit/revise/check
Section 4: create final copy/project

- Work on each section nightly until you have reached your completion date.

- Teachers give long-term assignments for students to enrich themselves in the curriculum and to improve their time management skills. If you follow this format, your child will meet the teacher's objectives efficiently...not the night before.

You must have the project completed two days prior to the assignment due date.

CHAPTER 3

Self-Image

Motivation

Motivation…maybe they just don't see the importance of being organized. In this case disorganization is a conscious choice. This is a behavior that can be changed. The child must be motivated to change that behavior. One of your responsibilities as a parent is to find that motivation for your child. You will have to think of examples of where and how organization is important in the real world. It is the child's responsibility to stay organized at school just like a job. You can give your child many hypothetical situations during your discussion to help them relate school to a career. What if a bank misplaced your deposit? What if a golfer forgot his putter before the Masters Tournament? "What if's" work great to teach motivation. You can also discuss with your child how academic success runs hand in hand with organization. If the child are struggling academically, organizational skills will help them improve their grades. You must reassure them that you believe in them and that you are here to help. Students who have the knowledge to be organized, but are not organized are very difficult to change. You and your child must establish a motivational/behavioral plan. Another name for a motivational system is a reward system.

How To Motivate Your Child

You probably already reward your child in the form of positive reinforcement and words of encouragement. If you are not doing this already, now would be a great time to start. A motivational system is designed to give a child a reward when the child reaches a predetermined goal within a predetermined amount of time. You must periodically check on the child whether it is daily, weekly, or monthly depending on the goals. Once the goals are reached, the system is reevaluated to give the child more responsibility and fewer rewards until the system is no longer needed. A new system may be put in place or it may not be needed. Although this type of motivation is mostly extrinsic, we must keep in mind that we are looking to obtain success. Once that goal is reached, you can modify the reward system. The child and parent together should decide upon the rewards. Smaller rewards should be for goals that can be easily reached. These rewards can be:

Verbal praise	Buy a candy bar
Pick favorite cereal	Throw the ball
Take out for ice cream	Play a board game
Read a book together	Ride bikes
Buy a soft drink	Build a snowman
Rent a movie	Go swimming

These are VERY important rewards because the child must be able to feel some success to serve as motivation to strive to reach for larger rewards. You then should have larger rewards for larger goals. Below are some larger rewards:

Take them to a ball game	Have friend spend the night
One hour of mom or dad time	Have a group of friends over
Go out to the movies	Camp out in living room
Purchase movie or game	Make cookies with mom or dad

You may notice that hugs are not a part of the reward lists. This is because hugs should be given after rewards AND consequences. Children need unconditional love and shouldn't be loved any more or any less because of their

PARENT TIP

Remember that you know your child and what motivates them best. If you need assistance with brainstorming motivational ideas, contact your child's teacher.

behavior. You must keep in mind that this system is meant to motivate your child to reach a goal and must be given careful thought. If the reward greatly overshadows the goal (success), it will be more difficult for the child to continue achieving success without a bigger, better reward.

For example, a 15-year-old boy who gets A's and B's is told that if he gets straight A's, then his parents will buy him a car for his sixteenth birthday. The boy is working for the car...not the goal. The boy will revert right back to getting A's and B's once he has the car unless another substantial reward is offered. This makes it difficult to have the boy experience success once the reward system ends.

The next scenario is a little different, but accomplishes the same goal. The boy is told that if he gets straight A's and a part-time job, the parents will match whatever money he earns towards the purchase of a car. This way the boy learns that he must reach the predetermined goal of straight A's and he must work hard outside of school to get HELP to purchase a car.

In the first scenario he is given a car for straight A's. There are no financial limits that are placed on the reward and the boy learns that good grades can get his parents to spend a lot of money.

In the second scenario the boy learns that buying a car is a large fiscal responsibility. He must get good grades, and there are some financial restraints put on him. His parents are only going to match what he makes. If he only makes $100 then he isn't going to be able to buy a car. If he makes $1000 then he can buy a car...but not much of one. The boy learns the meaning of a dollar and will begin to take pride in working...because he will see the fruit of his labor, in school and in the workplace.

It is very important that you revisit the reward system that you have created to check for success and make any needed modifications. This is a system that is in constant reevaluation. This system is meant to be a constant work-in-progress and can be changed if needed.

Confidence / Self-esteem

During our first few years of teaching, we coached seventh grade boys basketball together. One year we had a group of very talented athletes. Joey was a gifted athlete who was very quick, but did not have a lot of self-confidence. Once something did not go his way, he would get down on himself and not play to his full potential, thus hurting himself and his teammates. During practice, he would come off the floor with tears in his eyes when he made mistakes. Ben and I would talk about the positive aspects of his game on the floor and always give him the advice to never give up. We would joke around with him to get him to relax and remind him that basketball was just a game.

Our team posted an impressive record near the end of the season. Joey's playing time was limited. It was hard to trust his confidence on the floor. In the second to last game of the season, our team had a chance to avenge one of their earlier losses. The opposing team's fans were very unwelcoming and rude to our team. We could see it in our players' eyes that they were very nervous. After one quarter, we were losing by 10 points and the boys were not playing with any confidence. Then something happened that we hadn't seen all year. Joey began to be very verbal and positive during timeouts with his teammates. He had more confidence than we had ever seen and the other players started feeding off him. We immediately put Joey into the game. He sparked the team to make a miraculous comeback. With three seconds left Joey was fouled, with the score 43 to 44. We were losing by one point and he had a chance to win the game with two free throws. The other team called timeout. The boys came over to the bench and we talked to them about what we were going to do after Joey made both free throws. As the team came off the floor from the timeout, Joey could not take the pressure anymore and broke down. Tears streamed down his face so Alex knew he had to relax him. Alex asked, "Joey, are those new shoes?" Joey looked at Alex with a funny face, "Yeah, they're new!" Alex said, "It looks like they have helped your speed tonight and it's a good thing because you're going to need it in about three seconds." Joey said, "What are you talking about?" Alex responded, "When you make both free throws, those fans are going to try and chase you down." Joey smiled and wiped the tears from his face and headed to the free throw line. He made the first shot to tie the game. Joey's second shot went up and off the iron straight back toward Joey. The clock began to run and Joey went after the ball in a desperate attempt to get it. Joey was unable to get to the ball, yet one of his teammates caught the ball in mid-air and made the game-winning shot. Joey and his teammates ran off the floor with

some visiting fans chasing them. The security guard stopped
the fans from entering the locker room.

As coaches we learned how important persistence is with this
delicate topic. Kids need to know that they aren't always going
to be winners. That's all right, but they need to learn to believe
in themselves and never give up. It's funny that Alex and I don't
recall our final record that year, but we do vividly recall the
game we won with Joey.

It is possible your child just doesn't think that they can stay
organized. When you ask them about it, they tell you, "I try my
hardest, but I just can't seem to do it." That is a very big "cry for
help." Now however, the issue is confidence along with organization. They have tried all the ways they can to stay organized,
but cannot maintain a successful system. You should contact
your child's teacher and request a meeting to discuss what you
can do to help them.

Maybe it is too much for them to maintain the organizational
plan already in place. I don't mean to give up…not in any way,
but maybe give some assistance until they build confidence. The
key to this type of disorganization is positive reinforcement.
You must build their confidence so they believe that they can
do it. When they do something right or stay organized for a few
days you can reward them. This will help them to see that they
can be successful. Once their confidence is built and they are
successfully organized you can begin to help them to become
more independent.

On the next page are some simple ways to verbally praise
your child. These are very effective, but keep in mind being
involved and visible at all your child's activities are vital for their
confidence. A good daily question to ask your child is, "How
was your day at school?" When a child does something good, do
you know how to reply?

[Content]

TEACHING TIP

As teachers we wanted our students to feel comfortable and take academic risks. We gave struggling students modified assignments so they could experience success. We also got to know our students by building a positive rapport with them. We achieved this by taking an interest in them as people.

111 WAYS TO VERBALLY PRAISE A CHILD

Wow
Outstanding
Way to go
You've got it
Excellent
Great
Good
Neat
Well Done
Wonderful
Good Job
I knew you could do it
You are special
I am very proud of you
Remarkable
Super
Nice work
Looking good
Now you've got it
There you go
You are on top of it
You are smart
You are amazing
Hot dog

You are beautiful
You are a winner
You make me happy
Magnificent
Fantastic
Beautiful
You are important
Right on target
You are on your way
You are very nice
Spectacular
Stunning
You are impressive
Amazing
Fantastic
Fabulous
Extravagant
Brilliant
You are dazzling
You are astonishing
Marvelous
You are darling
You are inspirational
Extraordinary
Beautiful work

Good for you
Nothing can stop you now
Dynamite
Awesome
You are fantastic
You are precious
You've discovered the secret
Bingo
Great Discovery
You are responsible
You are fun
You are growing up
Wonderful performance
You tried hard
You gave 110%
You figured it out
You are a good listener
You mean a lot to me
You are correct
You are imaginative
You are creative
You are a genius

Now you are soaring

Bravo

I respect you

You earned it

You are sensational

You are phenomenal

A+ effort

A+ job

Hooray

You are unique

You care

What a helper

You are a leader

You've brightened my day

You are the best

You made my day

You mean the world to me

You are a good person

You make me laugh

You are a joy

A-OK

You are trustworthy

Perfect

Tremendous

You are efficient

I have confidence in you

You are a role model

I believe in you

Keep it up

Way to take the lead

You are cooperative

You have a gift

You are a good listener

That is your knack

Wonderful skill

You are a hard worker

Way to persevere

PARENT TIP

To build self-confidence provide your child with opportunities to be successful. The more times success is attained, the more self-confidence is built.

SUCCESS IS VITAL FOR
ANY CHILD TO BECOME A
SUCCESSFUL, HAPPY AND
INDEPENDENT LEADER.

CHAPTER 4

Consequences

Consequences Of Disorganization

The consequences can be very damaging if you do not choose to become organized. You will see that there are just as many negative effects as there are positive and they can affect you in school, work and in daily life.

The most apparent consequence is a child's academic successes and failures.

Some of the most devastating short-term effects of disorganization are listed below:

- Difficulty completing work
- Lowered grades due to assignments not turned in on time
- Displays how unimportant the assignment is to the student
- Students usually have hundreds of papers stuffed in their desk or locker
- They throw important papers away thinking they are unimportant
- Communication between parent and teacher is unclear
- Disorganized notes which results in low test scores
- Low self-confidence

Some devastating long-term effects of disorganized students are listed below:

- Students struggle to retain information and will fall behind academically
- Become less motivated in school
- Have social and emotional problems
- Affects their attitude outside of school
- Students will feel insecure and unsettled

If you really think about all of the stressors you have in your own life, how many are due to disorganization? Being organized and an efficient worker will reduce stress. You won't have to worry about dates, deadlines, or losing things. If you really focus on your organization, your stress will be minimized. You will be more confident in your individual decisions.

If students have a poor self-image, they think they cannot reach the end of the "road"…success. If they cannot reach success, they begin to find a way to stop going down that road. One way is to build a defense mechanism. Some kids will sabotage tasks deliberately because they don't believe success is attainable. This defense mechanism protects them from failing and being hurt. The good news is that all defense mechanisms can be reversed, no matter how extensive. They might just take more time and effort.

Another defense mechanism for children is to avoid the problem or in other words detour to another road. This detour can be anything that helps them feel successful. It can be the "road" of video games, sports, etc...In life, children will always encounter problems that they cannot avoid to reach their goal. It is important that children conquer those problems they encounter so they can stay on the road to life-long success. This road is very challenging and therefore is less traveled. Children must journey down the road that is less traveled so they can become successful and independent.

Independence is very significant in an individual's life. If a person is not independent, he or she will need constant help. A child will grow up to be dependent on other people. Those people will typically be one of the parents. If you do not work on the child's independence now, you will be supporting that child for the rest of your life in one way or another. Do you want to put forth the time and effort now or later?

CHILDREN MUST JOURNEY DOWN THE ROAD THAT IS LESS TRAVELED SO THEY CAN BECOME SUCCESSFUL AND INDEPENDENT.

CHAPTER 5

Benefits

Organizational Benefits

Success is the destination we all strive to reach. Most people will want to build on their success and will begin another journey or take on another challenge. Once you are organized, it will make every journey easier and more beneficial.

Many people have made organization a priority in their life and take time to organize their thoughts, jobs, tasks, etc... before they turn down the road to success. Once you have begun to achieve short-term success, you will notice lifestyle changes. Some lifestyle changes you will experience are less stress, more confidence, increased intelligence and increased work efficiency. Long-term success (which is the ultimate goal) will bring leadership and independence. Every parent wants his or her child to be an independent leader. As a parent and a teacher it makes us feel proud to see our children or our students exude these qualities. As administrators we require our employees to show these qualities and it all comes back to organization. If we have a disorganized student, child, employee, etc... it makes our jobs much more difficult. If we can teach them how to be organized, it will make our job easier and create a home, school or workforce of independent leaders who are all striving for the same goal...success!

Another benefit of organization is self-esteem. If children feel like they have the ability to conquer a task, they will be more motivated to try it. In most instances children will try to find a bigger challenge to conquer. Take video gaming, for example. Many kids know that they can beat a game if they continue to use what they have learned from the previous games they have played. The child will play the game for countless hours until they reach their goal of defeating the game. There's that word again...goal. They have confidence in themselves and their abilities. If you channel that confidence into their schoolwork, they could be much more successful. More success means more self-confidence and better self-esteem. Your child has now been nurtured to be happier and to have the confidence to take risks.

If you become organized, your work habits will improve which means that you will be more efficient and actually have more leisure time! If you can organize your tasks and supplies, then it is easier to complete assignments effectively. This makes doing homework and studying for tests and quizzes much more productive. The paper that you need to complete the assignment is in the correct spot, the notes that you need to study are available when needed, and the assignment specifics are clearly notated.

Comprehending and retaining knowledge is significant for academic success in school. This benefit is crucial because once you have organized yourself, you will learn to be able to apply knowledge to create things. In history class, you do not have to worry about finding the sheet of paper of dates to memorize because you already have the paper in the appropriate place. Instead, you can worry about the relevance of the dates and the events around that time period. You can apply that knowledge to evaluate certain situations in your life. Based on research these are high-level thinking skills that will help you to learn more efficiently. Why can you do this now and not before? Before you had to struggle to find the dates and wasted precious time when you could have been interpreting the dates and events instead. Can you do this and still be disorganized? No, not effectively because you spend more time trying to complete the same task. This will cause you to retain less information and learn less overall. You may not have the capacity to formulate higher level thinking questions or answers. If your child is organized, he or she will retain more information, ask or answer more thought provoking questions and use newfound knowledge to improve cognitive skills.

Organization will teach children the right way to be independent. They will learn to break down tasks systematically and solve them in an organized fashion. This will not happen unless they get the help they need. That help must come from the parent in the form of education…the education of organization.

> PEOPLE MUST MAKE
> ORGANIZATION A PRIORITY
> IN THEIR LIVES AND
> TAKE TIME TO ORGANIZE
> THEIR THOUGHTS, JOBS,
> TASKS, ETC...BEFORE
> THEY TURN DOWN THE
> ROAD TO SUCCESS.

CHAPTER 6

What Now?

What Now?

When Alex and I sat down to write this book, I thought about how I became organized. What triggered me to be motivated and successful? One memory of school I will never forget is my kindergarten conference night...

> ...My parents went to the school and I eagerly awaited their return of good news. To my surprise they came home with what I thought was devastating news. They told me my teacher said I was barely going to pass kindergarten. My teacher said I was smart enough, but didn't work very hard at school.

Now, were those the exact words that were said that night? I don't think so, but at age five, this was the way that I remembered it. Why would my parents tell me such a thing? I figured out later in my life that my parents had a wonderful way of motivating my two sisters and me. Looking back on that conference night, I think they knew exactly what they were doing the whole time.

This book contains many strategies that can help you as a parent teach your child to be successful. Thinking about where to start might feel overwhelming. Begin with a list of qualities or characteristics you would like your child to acquire. In other words, set a goal that you would like to reach to be successful. This will serve as a great motivational tool to help keep you focused. Goal-oriented people are more successful and better leaders. They are more successful because they are motivated, focused and confident. If you don't set goals, you won't have direction in your life; much like taking a road trip without a map. Leaders set goals for themselves and for others that are achievable. If goals are not achievable, you and the people around you will fail. For children to gain success, therefore, it is important to set goals with them.

I reminisced about a goal my mom wanted me to improve on when it came to organization. It must have been due dates with school work and using a calendar…

> …*I believe I was in the third grade when I remember we went to the store to buy poster board. My mother said we were going to make a calendar. This didn't make sense to me since we already had a larger calendar on our bulletin board. We bought six large poster boards and came home with them. I recall my mother sitting on the living room floor rewriting the calendar for the next six months onto six separate poster boards. When she was done, she called each one of us into the living room one by one. She made us write, using a fine tip marker, all of the practices, projects and days off school we would have in the next six months. She even made my dad sit down and do it, too. When everyone had written the events on the poster board calendar, she hung it on the large bulletin board. It was easily accessible.*

Wow! My mom was using teaching strategies that Alex and I had learned in college. Our family quickly learned to reference the calendar to keep our activities organized. It also made our parents more aware of what was going on in school. They could help us with projects and make sure we had them done on time. My mother's goal of organizing the family was achieved.

After you have your goal, you should make sure the physical things around your child are set up so the child can be successful. Go through the "Home Environment" section of our book again. We suggest you go in the order that we have described. If you feel your child has a good handle on the suggestions, proceed to the "School Environment" section. You must contact your child's teacher to discuss the new strategies you will be using from this book. Your child might start to develop routines and habits you had been hoping for, but you may still see the lack of confidence and self-esteem that you desire. I remember a time when I was in the same situation…

…When I was in the fourth grade. I was invited to practice football with our fifth and sixth grade flag football team. I was going to be the only fourth grader at the practice. I remember my mom driving me there. I had all the confidence in the world before we left home and then it hit me. During that drive to practice, I started to believe that there was no way I could compete with the older, more athletic kids. We arrived at the field and mom said, "Have fun, I'm going grocery shopping and by the time you're done, I'll be back." I said, "NO!" She said, "What do you mean, 'no'?" It must have been the look in my eyes because I didn't have to explain to her that I was terrified to play with the older boys. She pulled the mini van out of the parking lot and started to drive away. After a few minutes of silence, she began to tell me all the things that impressed her about me. She especially talked about sports and how someday I could do anything if I just tried really hard. As she talked and drove around the block, I began to gain confidence. She must have seen it again in my face because she pulled back into the parking lot at practice. She stopped the mini van and said, "I'll see you in an hour." I got out of the mini van with a renewed feeling of self-confidence.

This is the gift we have as parents. No one knows your child better than you. My mom knew I needed confidence and she delivered it with a successful strategy. The "Self-Image" part of our book offers strategies that can be used while you work on helping your child become successful at school and home. You do have a huge impact on what you say to your child. Think about some of the negative and positive things your parents said to you that you still remember.

Organization takes a lot of self-discipline. If students are disorganized, it affects so many aspects of their lives such as the ability to learn, grades, social life and self-esteem. Remember, it is never too late to change an attitude or a behavior. It does take a lot of hard work and energy. No success has ever been achieved without failures. Persistence will help you overcome these failures to change your child's life for the better. We hope from reading this book you gained the knowledge that will allow you to help your children reach their maximum potential. As teachers and parents, this has always been our goal.

Visit us at:
www.organizekids.com

Also, check out these other great
Kid Concoctions publications:

www.kidconcoctions.com